English for TRAVELING Abroad

한올출판사

Preface

21세기 Global 시대에 해외여행은 이제 누구에게나 열려있다. 중요한 것은 외국 여행할 때 얼마나 의사소통의 불편 없이 즐겁게 여행할 수 있느냐이다.

오랜 세월 학생들에게 관광영어를 가르치면서 얻은 경험과 해외 여행 경험을 바탕으로 꼭 필요한 영어표현들만을 엄선하여 해외 여행시 도움이 되도록 하였다.

1장에서는 출국 전 비행기 예약을 비롯하여 공항에서의 탑승 수속, 보안, 출국 심사 등의 출국 과정과 기내 서비스, 해외 도착 후 짐 찾기, 입국 심사, 세관 통과 등의 입국 절차, 그리고 환전에 필요한 영어 표현들을 다루었다.

2장에서는 해외 여행지에서 교통편, 호텔 투숙, 호텔 시설 이용, 퇴실, shopping 등에 관련된 표현들을 다루었다. 책 내용 및 구성에 있어서는 앞으로도 꾸준히 보완해 나가야 할 것이다.

세계는 넓다.

Go abroad and broaden your horizons!

끝으로, 책을 만든 동기를 부여 해준 제자들과 항상 격려해주는 가족들과 동료들, 그리고 수고하신 출판사분들께 감사의 말씀을 전하고 싶다.

2011년 5월

저자, 강 명 재

Contents

Part 1 | Traveling by Air

Part 2 | Staying at A Hotel

Part 1

Traveling by Air

Unit 1

Flight Reservations

WORDS & PHRASES

Reserve

Make a reservation

Book

Destination

Prefer

Have a preference

Available

One–way ticket

Round trip ticket

Return ticket

Flight

Window seat

Aisle seat

First class

Business class

Economy class

Departure

Arrival

BASIC EXPRESSIONS

- I'd like to reserve a flight.*
- I'd like to make a reservation for a flight.**
- I want to book a plane ticket.
- What is your destination, sir?
- Where would you like to fly, ma'am?
- Where will you be traveling, sir?
- I'll be traveling to Atlanta.
- I'm leaving for New York.
- I'm flying to Los Angeles.
- When will you be traveling, sir?
- When would you like to fly, ma'am?
- When are you planning to leave, ma'am?
- I'll leave on June 25th.
- I'm scheduled to leave on Friday, Jan. 7th.
- I'm planning to leave next Sunday, Feb. 3rd.

---

* I'd like to reserve a seat on a flight 와 같은뜻. 간단히 flight 만 흔히 쓰임.

** I'd like to make a plane reservation 과 같은뜻. I'd like to 대신 I want, I need 를 쓸 수 있다. I need를 쓸 때는 'I need help making my airline reservation.' 처럼 도움이 필요하다는 정도로 부드럽게 쓴다.

CONVERSATIONS

Dialogue 1

A : I'd like to make a plane reservation.

B : All right, ma'am. What is your destination?

A : I will be traveling to Atlanta, Georgia.

B : When are you scheduled to leave?

A : I'm scheduled to leave on July 7th.

B : What time would you prefer, morning or afternoon?

A : I prefer morning.

B : We have two flights available in the morning. One at 9 AM and the other at 11:30 AM.

A : I'd like the one at 11:30 AM.

B : I can book that for you right now.

Translation 우리말 해석을 보며 영어표현을 다시 연습한다.

A : 비행기표 예약하고 싶습니다.

B : 목적지는 어디신지요?

A : 미국 Atlanta 입니다.

B : 언제 떠나실 건가요?

A : 7월 7일입니다.

B : 오전 오후 어느 쪽이 좋으신가요?

A : 오전이 좋습니다.

B : 오전에 두편이 가능합니다.
9시와 11시 30분입니다.

A : 11시 30분으로 하겠습니다.

B : 지금 바로 예약해드리겠습니다.

Dialogue ❷

A : I want to make my airline reservation to Auckland, New Zealand.

B : Sure. When are you planning to leave?

A : I'll leave July 20th and be back July 30th.

B : All right. Would you like a one way ticket?

A : No, I'd like a round trip ticket.

B : What class would you like?

A : Economy class, please.

B : Does it matter to you if you leave in the morning or afternoon?

A: No, I can leave at either time.

B : When you return, is a morning or afternoon return flight preferable for you?

A : I would like a morning return flight better.

B : I'll put you on a morning flight, then.

Translation 우리말 해석을 보며 영어표현을 다시 연습한다.

A : 뉴질랜드의 오클랜드 가는 항공편 예약하고 싶습니다.

B : 네, 언제 출발할 예정이신지요?

A : 7월 20일 출발해서 30일에 돌아옵니다.

B : 편도표를 원하십니까?

A : 아니요, 왕복표를 원합니다.

B : 좌석 등급은 무엇으로 하시겠습니까?

A : 일반석으로 해주세요.

B : 오전과 오후 출발 상관 있으신가요?

A : 아니요, 둘 다 괜찮습니다.

B : 오실 땐, 오전 오후 중 언제가 좋으신가요?

A : 올 때는 오전 비행편이 더 좋습니다.

B : 그럼 오전 비행편으로 해 드리겠습니다.

Dialogue ❸

A : Could I get a seat to Christchurch next Friday morning.

B : Certainly, Ma'am. We have one flight available at 10 AM.

A : How much is the fare of economy class?

B : It's $850 for one-way, $150 round trip.

A : I'd like a round trip ticket.

B : May I have your name and phone number, please?

A : I'm Kang Susie, Kang is last name*. Phone number is 02-321-1234.

B : Your reservation is made on flight UA 707 to Christchurch at 10 AM on the 7th of July. Your reservation number is 32233. Please reconfirm** your reservation 72 hours before departure.

---

* 우리나라 성(last name)과 이름(first name)의 혼동을 피하기 위해 확인해 주는 것이 좋다.

** 재확인하다.

Translation 우리말 해석을 보며 영어표현을 다시 연습한다.

A : 다음 금요일 오전에 크라이스트처치 좌석 예약 할 수 있나요?

B : 물론이죠. 오전 10시에 비행편이 하나 있습니다.

A : 일반석 항공 요금은 얼마인가요?

B : 편도 850달러, 왕복 150달러 입니다.

A : 왕복표로 하고 싶습니다.

B : 성함과 전화번호 어떻게 되시나요?

A: 강수지입니다. Kang이 성입니다. 전화번호는 02-321-1234 입니다.

B : 7월 7일 오전 10시 출발, UA 707 편으로 예약되었습니다. 예약번호는 32233입니다.

출발 72시간 전에 예약을 재확인 하시기 바랍니다.

◀ Airline Ticketing Counter

FURTHER EXPRESSIONS

1. I am planning a trip and need help making my airline reservation.

2. Could you help me make a plane reservation?

3. Where are you traveling to on your trip?

4. Would you prefer a morning or afternoon departure?

5. On your return flight, do you have a preference as to morning or afternoon?

6. What is your preference?

7. Either morning or afternoon would work for me.

8. I would prefer to return in the morning.

9. I'll put you on a morning flight.

10. Your reservation has been made.

11. I'd like to confirm my reservation.

▶ 여행시 공항 가기 전에 꼭 준비해야 할 서류는 여권과 입국허가증(visa) 그리고 비행기ticket(e-ticket). 이 3가지가 있어야 check-in counter에서 탑승권 (boarding pass) 발급 가능!

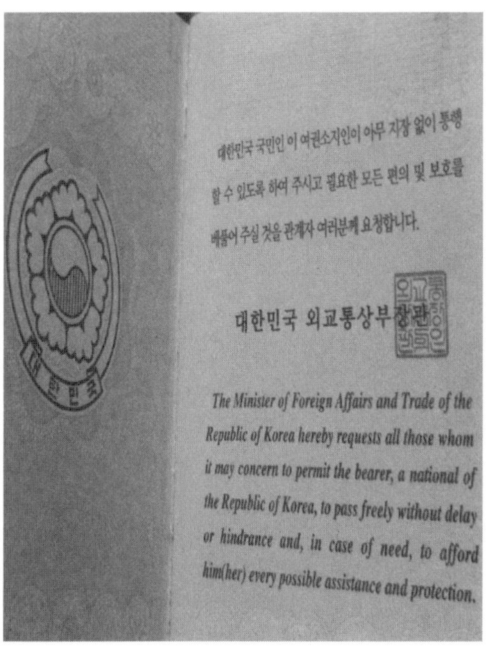

◀ 대한민국 여권의 첫 페이지

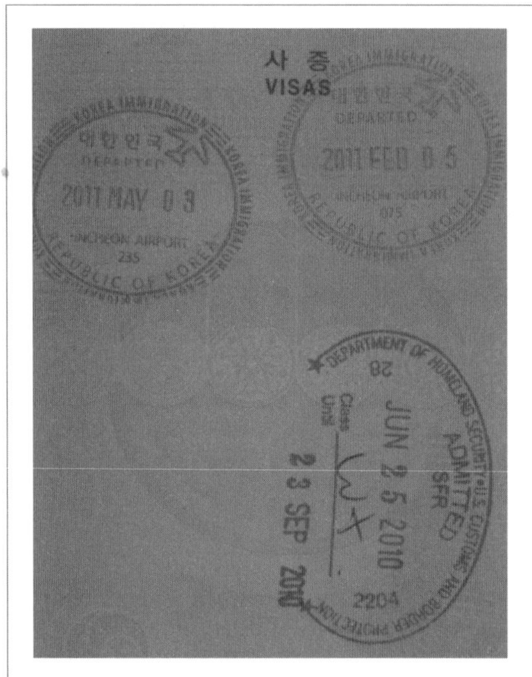

◀ 여권에 찍힌 출국 및 입국 심사 통과 확인 도장!

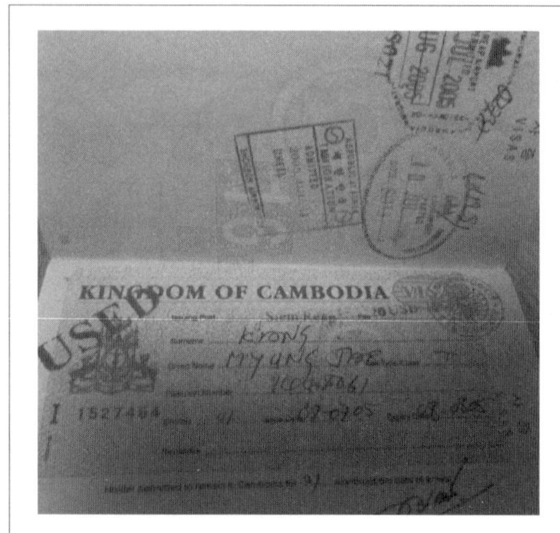

▲ 캄보디아 Visa

▼ 중국 Visa

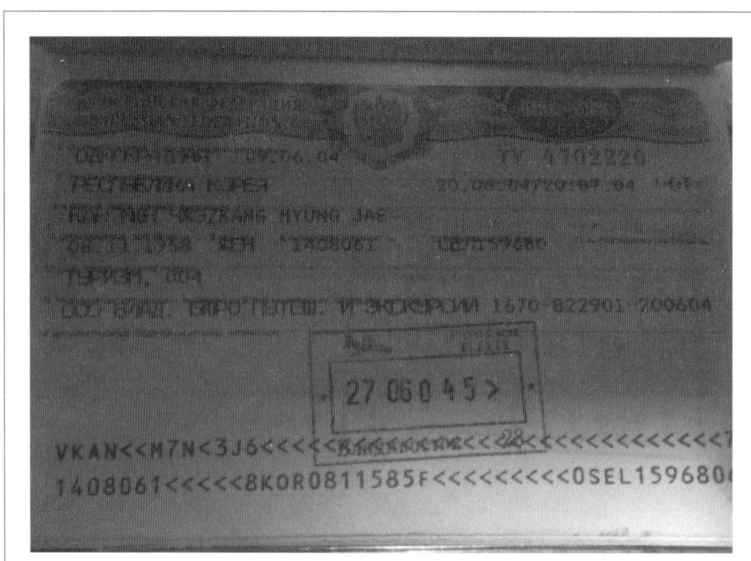

TASK

❶ 본문의 나온 대화를 짝과 서로 연습해 보고 상황 별로 보지 않고 발표할 수 있도록 한다.

❷ 인터넷에서 미국과 우리나라의 비자 면제 프로그램 (visa waiver program)으로 3개월 무비자 여행이 가능한 ESTA(Electronic System for Travel Authorization: 미국 전자 여행 허가제) 에 대해 알아 본다.

Memo

Unit 2

Departure Procedures

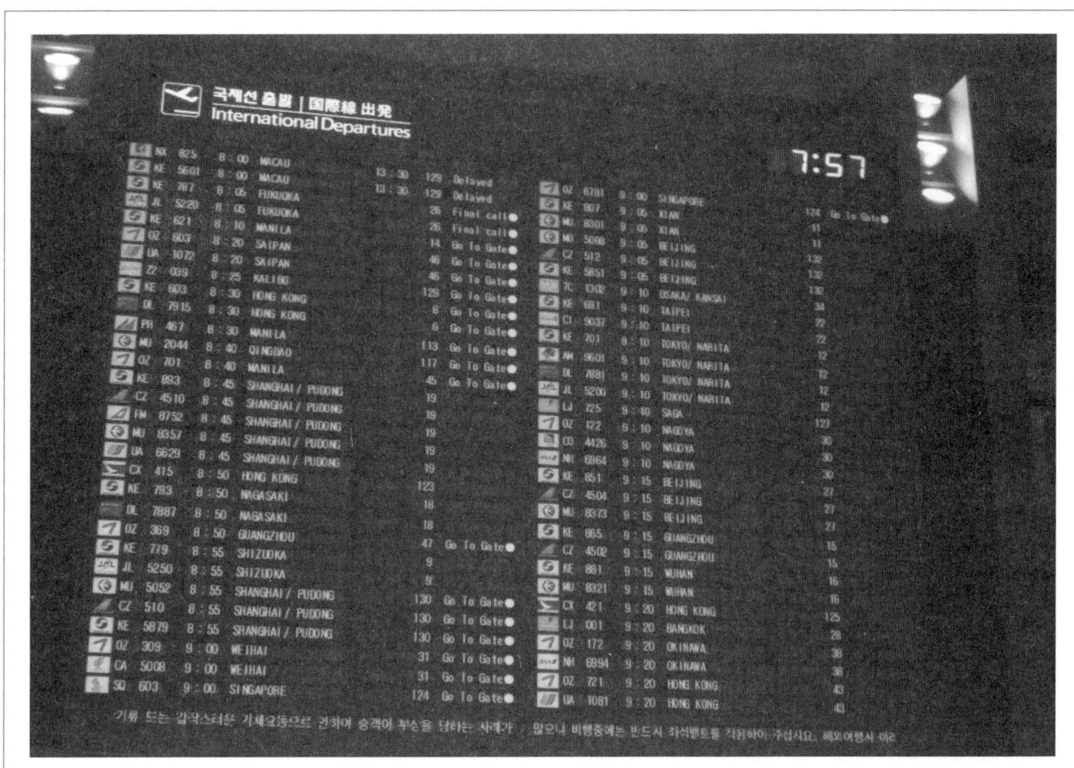

WORDS & PHRASES

Departure

Check–in

Baggage

Luggage

Baggage allowance

Weigh

Extra weight

Scale

Baggage claim tag

Passport

Boarding pass

Airport tax

Carry–on

Security guard

Security processing

Passport control

Emigration

Embarkation card

Disembarkation card

Baggage cart

Porter

CIQ (Customs, Immigration, Quarantine)

BASIC EXPRESSIONS

- I'd like to check in.
- Your passport and ticket, please.
- Do you have any baggage to check?
- Yes, I have one bag.
- Put it on the scale, please.
- Here's your boarding pass.

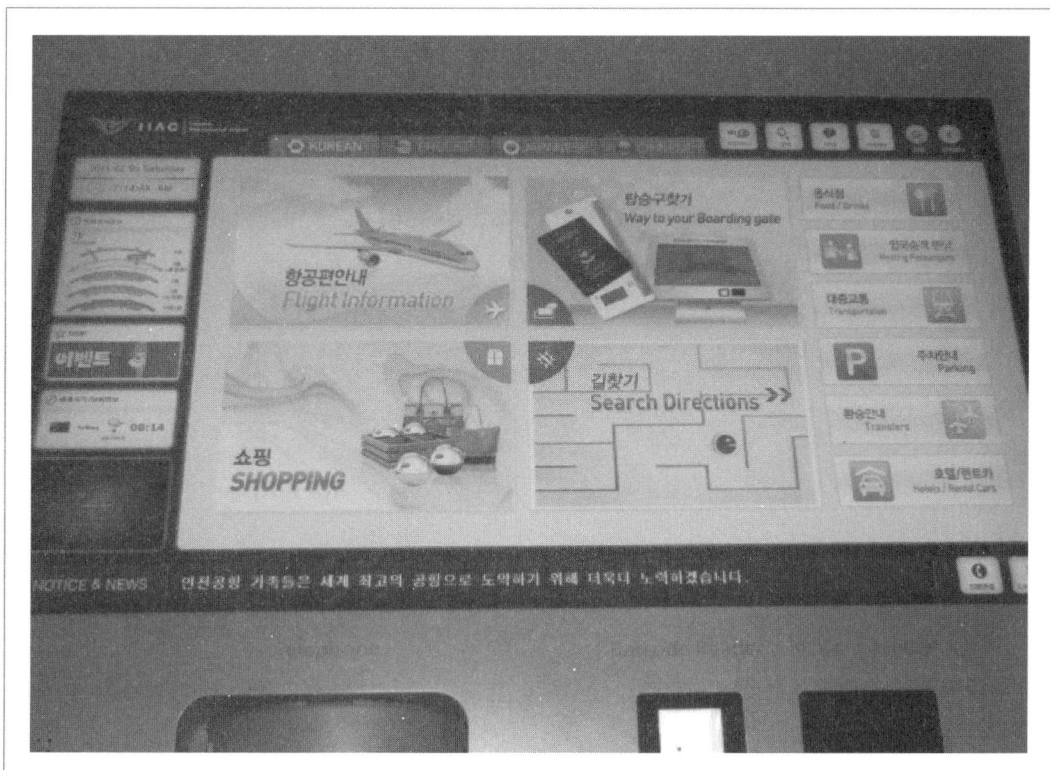

CONVERSATIONS

Dialogue ①

A : I'd like to check in.

B : All right. Your passport and ticket, please.*

A : Here they are.**

B : Any baggage to check***?

A : No. I only have a carry-on.****

B : Okay. Here's your boarding pass.

---

* Could you show me your passport and ticket? 또는 May I see your passport and ticket? 의 줄임형.

** Here you are와 같은 뜻.

*** Is there any baggage to check? 또는 Do you have any baggage to check?를 줄여서 간략히 사용.

**** carry-on(baggage or luggage)은 기내용 가방.

Translation 우리말 해석을 보며 영어표현을 다시 연습한다.

A : 탑승 수속을 밟고 싶은데요.

B : 네. 여권과 항공권을 보여 주세요.

A : 여기 있습니다.

B : 탁송하실 수하물이 있으세요?

A : 없습니다. 휴대용 짐 하나뿐 이에요.

B : 알겠습니다. 여기 탑승권 입니다.

Dialogue ❷

A : Is this the check-in counter for Air New Zealand?

B : Yes, it is.

A : I'd like an aisle seat, please.

B : I'm sorry. There is only one window seat left.

A : I'll take the window seat, then.

B : All right, here's your boarding pass.

Translation 우리말 해석을 보며 영어표현을 다시 연습한다.

A : 여기가 뉴질랜드 항공 체크인 카운터입니까?

B : 네, 그렇습니다.

A : 통로쪽 좌석을 주세요.

B : 죄송합니다. 창문 쪽 좌석 하나밖에 남아 있지 않은데요.

A : 그럼 창문 쪽으로 해 주세요.

B : 네, 탑승권 여기 있습니다.

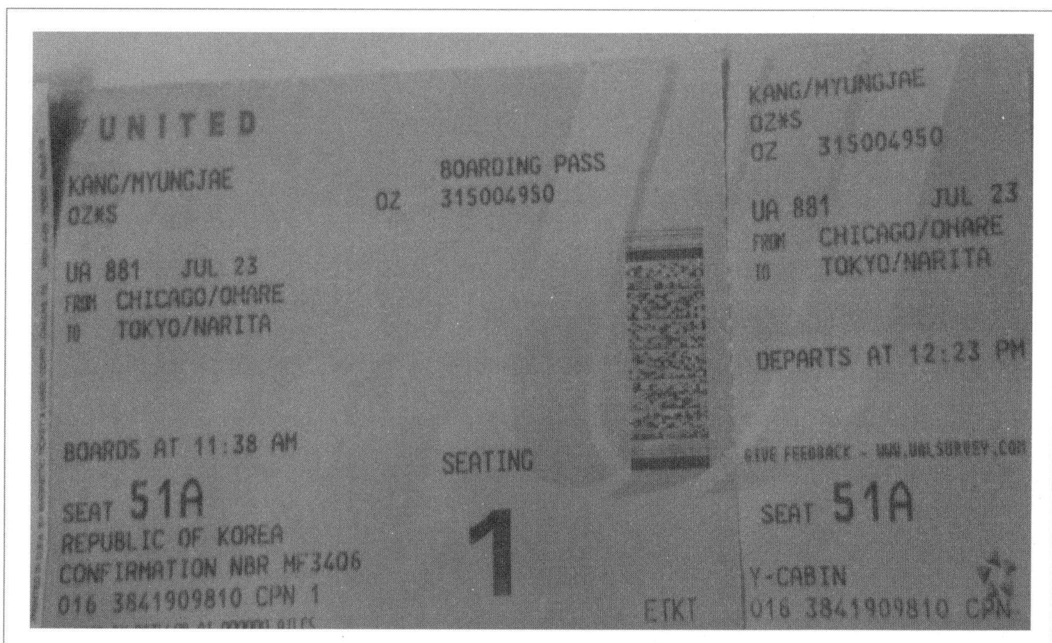

Dialogue ❸

A : I'd like to check this baggage.

B : All right. Please put it on the scale.

A : I'm afraid it might be over the limit.*

B : No. It's O.K. Here's your baggage claim ticket.**

A : Thank you. Can I take this one on with me?

B : No problem. One carry–on is allowed.

* 한도초과

** baggage claim tag (수하물 표)

Translation 우리말 해석을 보며 영어표현을 다시 연습한다.

A : 이 짐을 탁송하고 싶은데요.

B : 네. 저울 위에 올려 놓으세요.

A : 중량이 초과하지 않을는지 모르겠군요.

B : 아니예요. 괜찮습니다. 수하물 인환증 여기 있습니다.

A : 감사합니다. 이것은 직접 가지고 타도 되겠죠?

B : 아무 문제없습니다. 기내용 가방은 하나만 허용됩니다.

▲ 요즈음은 self check-in kiosk*가 있어 줄을 서지 않고도 신속하게 수속 할 수 있다. 안내에 따라 그대로 하면 된다. 전자 여권을 가지고 있는 경우에 가능하며 예약 후 e-ticket이 있어야 가능하다. 본인의 항공편 예약번호 입력하고 전자 여권을 scan 한 후 원하는 좌석을 touch screen 으로 선택하면 탑승권이 나온다. 부칠 짐이 있으면 자동 발권 후 가까운 곳에 마련된 창구에서 부치면 시간을 절약할 수 있다.

* 무인 탑승 수속 전자 단말기

▲ 여권과 탑승권을 항공사 직원에게 제시하고 드디어
일반석 통로를 통해 비행기 탑승!

Dialogue ④

A : What should I do* if my baggage is over the limit?

B : You must pay for the extra weight.**

A : How much do I have to pay for the extra weight?

B : 10 dollars per Kilogram.

A : I see. Will this bag fit*** as a carry-on?

B : I think so.

---

* 어떻게 할까요? 'what shall I do' 로 바꾸어 쓸 수 있다.

** 초과중량

*** fit: 동사로 쓰여 '딱 들어 맞다', '규격에 맞는다' 는 뜻.
Does this suit fit you? 에서는 이 양복이 몸에 딱 맞는냐는 뜻.

Translation 우리말 해석을 보며 영어표현을 다시 연습한다.

A : 내 짐이 중량 초과되면 어떻게 해야 되나요?

B : 초과분에 대한 요금을 내시면 됩니다.

A : 초과분에 대한 요금은 얼마입니까??

B : 킬로그램당 10 달러입니다.

A : 알겠습니다. 이 가방은 기내용 규격에 맞을까요?

B : 괜찮을 것 같습니다.

◀ Check-in 후, 국제선 탑승입구에서 여권 제시하고 출국장으로 들어가면 바로 보안 검색대(Security Control)가 나온다.

▲ 출국장. 안으로 들어가는 여행객 너머로 보안검색대가 보인다.

▲ 보안 검색대, 출국 심사대의 간단한 출국심사 후 확인 도장 받고 국제선 탑승구를 향해 출발~ 바로 앞에 세금 (Tax) 내지 않고 물건 살 수 있는 면세점 (duty free shop) 도 보이네요.

Dialogue ⑤

A : Excuse me, is this the right* terminal for international flights?

B : Yes, it is.

A : Which way is it to Gate 135, please?

B : It's just around the corner**

A : Thank you.

B : Oh, wait a minute. I'm sorry, I was mistaken. Gate 135 is in the opposite*** direction.

---

* 여기서는 right가 오른쪽이 아니라 '맞는' 의 의미로 쓰임.

** just around the corner 는 바로 앞의 거리가 가까운 곳을 뜻하며 'My birthday is just around the corner.' 에서 처럼 바로 임박한 때를 나타내기도 한다.
'Just' 대신 'right'를 써서 'Our Independence day is right around the corner.'(독립기념일이 얼마 남지 않았다)로 써도 된다.

*** opposite 는 반대편, 맞은편의 뜻.

Translation

우리말 해석을 보며 영어표현을 다시 연습한다.

A : 실례합니다. 여기가 국제선 청사 맞습니까?

B : 네, 맞습니다.

A : 135번 탑승 출구가 어느 쪽에 있나요?

B : 바로 모퉁이 돌면 있습니다.

A : 감사합니다,

B : 잠깐만요. 제가 잘못 알았군요. 135번 탑승 출구는 반대편에 있습니다.

FURTHER EXPRESSIONS

1. Excuse me, could you direct me to Gate 125?

2. Go straight this way.

3. Excuse me. How do I get to Gate125, please?

4. Go this way and turn to the right.

5. Excuse me, where is Gate125?

6. It's right over there.

7. You're five kilos over the weight limit.

8. Your baggage weight exceeds the baggage allowance.

9. Your baggage weighs over the limit.

10. You have to pay for the extra weight.

11. How much will that extra weight be?

12. That will be 50 dollars.

13. I'll pay for that.

14. Please go to customs and immigration, then, proceed to Gate 125.

TASK

❶ 인터넷에서 'self check-in kiosk'에 대하여 사용법을 자세히 알아보도록 한다.

❷ 출입국 자동심사 (automatic immigration clearance)에 대해 알아보도록 한다.

❸ 다음의 arrival card (disembarkation card)를 본인의 이름으로 작성 해 본다.

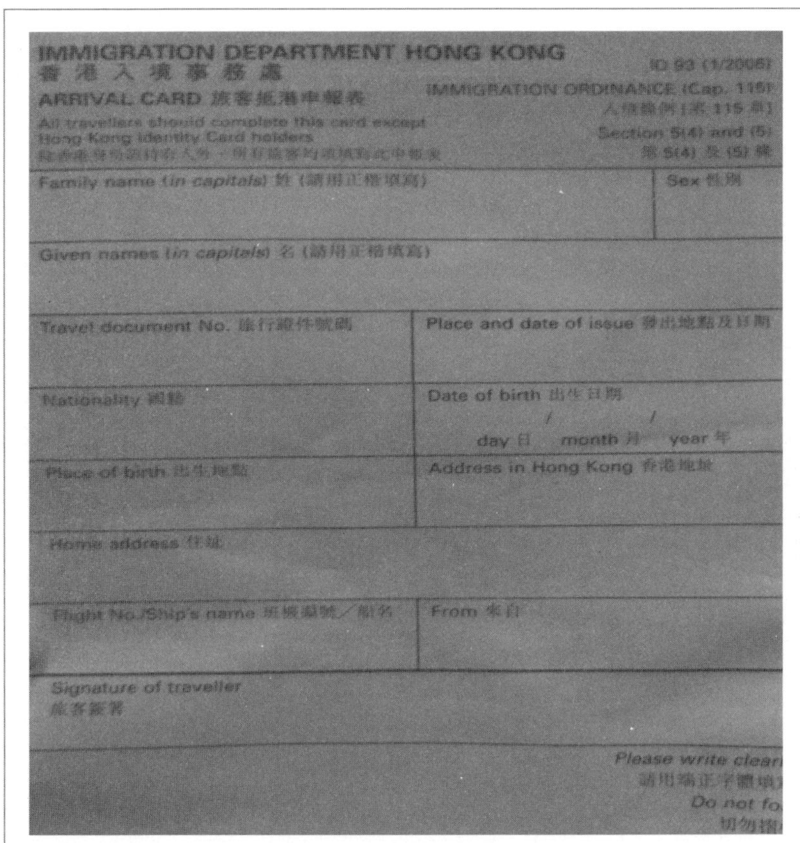

IMMIGRATION DEPARTMENT HONG KONG
香港入境事務處
ARRIVAL CARD 旅客抵港申報表
All travellers should complete this card except Hong Kong Identity Card holders
ID 93 (1/2006)
IMMIGRATION ORDINANCE (Cap. 115)
Section 5(4) and (5)

Family name (in capitals) | Sex
Given names (in capitals)
Travel document No. | Place and date of issue
Nationality | Date of birth (day / month / year)
Place of birth | Address in Hong Kong
Home address
Flight No./Ship's name | From
Signature of traveller
Please write clearly
Do not fold

◀ 성, 이름, 성별, 여권번호, 생년 월일, 국적, 출생지, 집주소, 목적지 주소, 항공편, 출발지명 기록 후 서명한다. 입국카드는 접지 않도록 주의한다.

Memo

Unit 3

In-flight Service

WORDS & PHRASES

Boarding time

Boarding gate

Captain

Cockpit

Flight attendant

Cabin

Cabin announcement

Cabin crew

Flight crew

Steward (Stewardess)

Overhead compartment

Tray table

Recline

Upright position

Seat pocket

Devices

Valuables

Belongings

Altitude, Longitude

Lavatory

Occupied

Vacant

In–flight meal

Airsickness

Passenger control unit

Duty free goods

Duty free allowance

Deplane

Ground staff

Stopover

Transit

Connecting flights

Disembarkation card

CIQ (Customs, Immigration, Quarantine) form

BASIC EXPRESSIONS

- May I have your attention, please?
- Passengers boarding Korean Air flight number 235 leaving for Atlanta are kindly requested to board through Gate 125.
- Delta Airlines announces the departure of flight 535 to New York.
- To prepare to take off, all portable electronic devices such as cellular phones, CD players, and laptop computers must be turned off until the seat belt sign goes off.
- On behalf of United Airlines, Captain Thomas and your crew, welcome aboard!
- Keep your bag under the seat in front of you.
- Please put your bag in the overhead compartment.
- Please fasten your seatbelt.
- Please return your seat to the upright position.
- You may unfasten your seatbelt.
- What would you like to have, chicken or beef?
- Would you help me fill out this form?
- We're now approaching JFK International Airport.
- We're landing shortly.
- Please remain in your seat until the aircraft comes to a complete stop.

◆ Overhead compartment: 짐이나 옷 등은 머리 위 선반에 안전하게 넣는다.

CONVERSATIONS

Dialogue ①

A : What would you like to drink, ma'am?

B : Seven-up*, please.

A : What would you prefer, meat or fish?

B : I'll have fish, please.

A : Anything else?

B : Can I have some white wine, please?

* seven-up은 우리나라 cider를 생각하면 된다.
'cider'라고 하면 'apple cider'를 주는데 약간의 알코올이 들어간 음료로 우리가 생각하는 cider와는 거리가 있다.

Translation 우리말 해석을 보며 영어표현을 다시 연습한다.

A : 음료 뭘 드시겠습니까?

B : 세븐 업 주세요.

A : 육류와 생선 중 어느것 선호하시나요?

B : 생선주세요.

A : 다른 것은요?

B : 백포도주 마실 수 있나요?

▲ One of the best in-flight menu: Korean mixed rice (비빔밥)

Dialogue ❷

A : I feel airsick. Could you bring me some pills?

B : I'll bring them to you right away.

A : Thanks.

B : Please take these pills and try to get some sleep.

A : I feel chilly. One more blanket please.

B : Here you are.

Translation 우리말 해석을 보며 영어표현을 다시 연습한다.

A : 멀미가 나는데요. 약 좀 가져다 주시겠습니까?

B : 곧 갖다 드리지요.

A : 감사합니다.

B : 약 드시고 좀 주무세요.

A : 추운데요. 담요 하나 더 갖다 주세요.

B : 여기 있습니다.

▲ Flight attendant (Stewardess)

Dialogue ❸

A : How can I turn off the light?

B : Just push this button here.

A : Thanks. What's the local time in LA now?

B : It's 7 AM.

A : What's the actual flying time to LA?

B : It's almost 10 hours. We'll get there in an hour.*

* in an hour: 한시간 후에 within an hour: 한시간 이내에

Translation 우리말 해석을 보며 영어표현을 다시 연습한다.

A : 전등은 어떻게 켜나요?

B : 여기 버튼을 누르세요.

A : 감사합니다. LA 현지시간은 몇 시죠?

B : 아침 7시 입니다.

A : 실제 비행시간은 얼마나 되나요?

B : 약 10시간입니다. 1시간 후엔 도착합니다.

FURTHER EXPRESSIONS

Captain's Announcement

Ladies & gentlemen. On behalf of Delta Airlines, Captain Thomas and your crew, welcome aboard! It's a pleasure to have you with us. We will be flying at an altitude of 11,000 feet, with a ground speed of 580 miles per hour. Our flying time to New York will be 12 hours and thirty minutes after take-off. Please fasten your seat belt. Our cabin attendants are happy to assist you. Please enjoy your flight. Thank you.

Captain's Final Announcement

Ladies & gentlemen. We're approaching JFK International Airport. Please fasten your seat belt and return your seat and tray table to the upright position. All portable electronic devices must be turned off until the aircraft is parked at the gate. It has been our pleasure serving you today, and we wish you a pleasant stay in New York. Thank you.

Transit Information

Ladies & gentlemen. Passengers continuing on to LA have to change aircraft here in Tokyo. Please be sure to take all your belongings with you when you deplane. After you deplane, please follow the guidance of our ground staff. Thank you.

TASK

❶ 본문의 나온 대화를 짝과 서로 연습해 보고 상황 별로 보지 않고 발표할 수 있도록 한다.

❷ 인터넷에서 항공사 별 기내 안내 방송을 찾아보고 항공사 별로 다른 점이 있는지 찾아 본다.

Memo

Unit 4

Arrival Procedures

WORDS & PHRASES

Baggage claim area

Conveyor belt

Carousel

Quarantine office

Immigration check

Security check

Baggage retrieval

Customs clearance

Entry visa

Status of sojourn

Personal belongings

Airport administration office

Transit passengers

Connecting flights

Layover

Stopover

Lost and found

BASIC EXPRESSIONS

- Where can I pick up my baggage?
- Where is the baggage claim area?
- Where is the immigration office?
- May I see your passport and arrival card?
- What's the purpose of your visit?
- I'm here on business.
- I'm here on vacation.
- I'm here for studying.
- How long will you stay in America?
- Where are you going to stay?
- Where can I clear customs?
- Your customs declaration form, please.
- How much did you pay for the perfume?
- I paid 50 dollars at the duty free shop.
- Everything is cleared.
- Enjoy your stay in New York.
- We're waiting for our connecting flight to Chicago.

Conversations

Baggage Claim: Dialogue ①

A : Excuse me, where do I pick up my baggage?

B : You are looking for the baggage claim area?

A : Yes.

B : It's right over there, where that carousel is turning.

A : Aha, is that it? Thanks a lot.

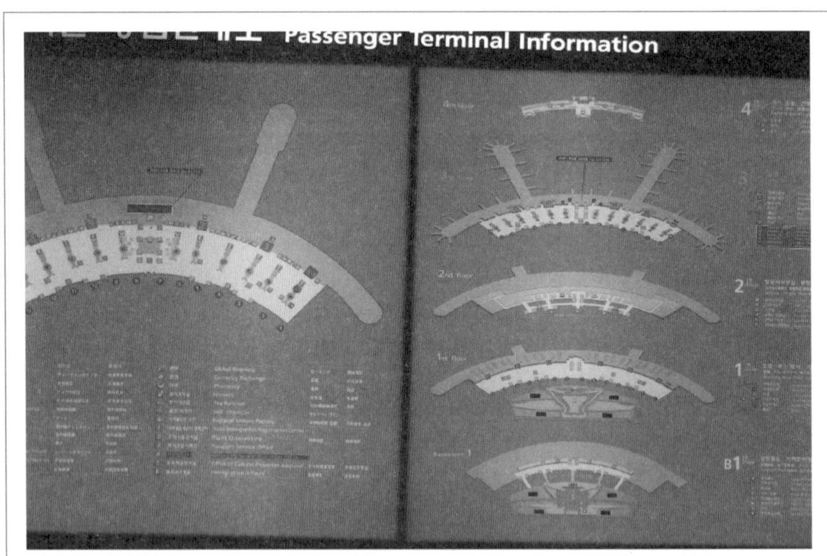

▲ 공항 여객 터미널 정보

Translation 우리말 해석을 보며 영어표현을 다시 연습한다.

A : 실례지만, 수하물은 어디서 찾습니까?

B : 짐 찾는 곳을 찾으시는군요?

A : 네.

B : 바로 저기입니다. 저 회전대가 돌고 있는 곳 말입니다.

A : 아, 바로 저기군요. 감사합니다.

▲ Baggage claim area: 'Conveyor belt' 또는 Carousel' 에서 나오는 짐을 찾는다.

▲ Carousel에서 짐을 찾아 cart에 싣는다.

▲ Quarantine Inspection: 검역 할 때 열이 나거나 구토 증상이 있으면 격리 함.

Baggage Claim: Dialogue ❷

A : I can't find my baggage, What should I do?

B : Well, I'll check on it.

B : Do you have the baggage claim ticket?

A : Yes, here it is.

A : Can you help me find my baggage, please?

B : Sure.

▲ Customer Service desk: baggage claim 등 여러가지 정보에 관해 물을 수 있다.

Translation

우리말 해석을 보며 영어표현을 다시 연습한다.

A : 내 짐이 보이지를 않습니다. 어떻게 하면 되죠?

B : 제가 알아 봐 드리죠.

B : 수하물 표를 갖고 계십니까?

A : 네, 여기 있습니다.

A : 제 짐 찾는 걸 좀 도와 주시겠습니까?

B : 그러죠.

▲ Baggage Claim Area

Immigration: Dialogue ①

A : What's the purpose of your visit to the United States?

B : I'm here on business.*

A : How long will you be staying?

B : For a couple of weeks.

A : Where are you going to stay?

B : I'm going to stay at the Hilton Hotel.

▲ 입국심사대

* on business: 사업상, on holiday(vacation): 휴가로

Translation

우리말 해석을 보며 영어표현을 다시 연습한다.

A : 미국 방문 목적이 무엇입니까?

B : 사업차 왔습니다.

A : 얼마 동안 머무실 건가요?

B : 한 2주일 정도 있을 겁니다.

A : 어디에 묵으실 겁니까?

B : 힐튼 호텔에 묵을 겁니다.

Immigration: Dialogue ❷

A : Do you have a return ticket*?

B : Yes, here it is.

A : What's your final destination in the States?

B : Atlanta, Georgia.

A : How much money are you carrying with you?

B : One thousand dollars in traveler's checks.

---

* return ticket = round trip ticket.(왕복표, 귀국용표)

Translation

우리말 해석을 보며 영어표현을 다시 연습한다.

A : 귀국 비행기표를 갖고 있습니까?

B : 네, 여기 있습니다.

A : 미국에서 최종 목적지는 어디입니까?

B : 조지아주 아틀란타입니다.

A : 현금은 얼마나 갖고 계십니까?

B : 여행자 수표로 천 달러 갖고 있습니다.

Customs: Dialogue ①

A : Do you have anything to declare?

B : No, I have nothing to declare.

A : What do you have in these bags?

B : Nothing special. Just my personal belongings.

A : Do you have any gifts or souvenirs?

B : Yes, I have some Korean ginseng for my American friend.

Translation 우리말 해석을 보며 영어표현을 다시 연습한다.

A : 신고하실 물건이 있습니까?

B : 아뇨. 신고할 것이 아무것도 없습니다.

A : 이 가방에는 뭐가 들어 있습니까?

B : 별 것 아닙니다. 저의 개인 소지품들 뿐입니다.

A : 선물이나 기념품 종류를 갖고 계십니까?

B : 네. 미국인 친구에게 줄 한국 인삼이 있습니다.

▲ 신고할 것이 없으면 Nothing to declare (green zone) 로 통과 한다.

Customs: Dialogue ②

A : Your customs declaration, please.

B : Here it is.

A : Will you please open this bag?

B : Sure.

A : Do you have more money than you have declared on this form?

B : No, I don't.

▲ Immigration check 한 후에 customs clearance (세관검사) 통과 한다.

Translation

우리말 해석을 보며 영어표현을 다시 연습한다.

A : 세관 신고서를 주십시오.

B : 여기 있습니다.

A : 이 가방 좀 열어 주시겠습니까?

B : 그러죠.

A : 신고하신 금액보다 더 많은 돈을 갖고 계십니까?

B : 아닙니다.

Connecting Flights: Dialogue ❶

A : Excuse me, what flight are you waiting for?

B : I'm waiting for my plane to get ready to go.

A : What do you mean?

B : I'm a transit passenger. My plane has stopped over at this airport for refueling.

A : I see. Where is your plane bound?

B : New York.

▲ 갈아타는 승객들은 탑승권이 없으면 Connecting flight (연결 편 항공)의 boarding pass를 transit check in counter 에서 다시 수속해야 한다.

Translation 우리말 해석을 보며 영어표현을 다시 연습한다.

A : 실례지만, 어느 항공편을 기다리고 계십니까?

B : 비행기가 떠날 준비를 갖추기를 기다리고 있어요.

A : 무슨 말씀인지?

B : 저는 통과 여객입니다. 우리 비행기가 재급유를 받기 위해서 이 공항에 잠시 머물고 있습니다.

A : 알겠습니다. 어디로 가는 비행기입니까?

B : 뉴욕입니다.

▲ Connecting flights를 기다리는 transit passengers는 탑승권 수속을 먼저 확인하고 여유 시간에 면세점에서 쇼핑도 하고 마사지 등도 즐길 수 있다.

Connecting Flights: Dialogue ❷

A : How do I know when to board?

B : There will be an announcement for boarding.

A : How long do we have to wait for our connecting flight?

B : About three hours.

A : What are all those people doing here?

B : We're having a layover* for our connection** to Boston.

▲ 환승 비행편을 타기 위한 환승 버스 안내

---

* layover = stopover(도중하차, 경유지)

** connection = connecting flight(연결비행편)

Translation 우리말 해석을 보며 영어표현을 다시 연습한다.

A : 탑승을 언제 하는지 어떻게 알죠?

B : 탑승하라는 안내 방송이 나올 겁니다.

A : 연결편 비행기를 타려면 얼마나 기다려야 합니까?

B : 약 두 시간 정도.

A : 이분들은 모두 여기서 뭘 하고 있는 겁니까?

B : 우리는 보스톤행 연결 비행기편을 타려고 잠시동안 기다리고 있는 겁니다.

▲ 홍콩 공항에서 환승객들(transfer passengers)이 기다리고 있다.

FURTHER EXPRESSIONS

1. May I see your passport and disembarkation card?

2. What kind of work do you do?

3. I work for a trading company.

4. My bag isn't coming out. Will you check it for me?

5. Could I see your baggage claim tag?

6. What does your bag look like?

7. It's blue, about this size.

8. It should be coming around on that carousel soon.

9. Please wait a little.

10. It's coming out now.

11. Please be sure to check if it's yours.

12. Certainly, I will.

▲ 도쿄 나리타 공항의 커피전문점, 스타벅스.

▲ 혹시 수하물 등을 분실 하였을 경우 분실물 센터 (Lost and Found)을 찾아가면 된다.

TASK

❶ 인천 국제 공항의 출국과 입국 순서를 인터넷에서 찾아 조사해 본다.

❷ Transit Passenger 중 Boarding pass가 없는 경우는 공항 도착 후 어디로 가서 수속을 밟아야 하는지 알아 본다.

❸ 수하물을 분실하였을 때는 어떻게 하여야 하는가?

Memo

Unit 5

Money Exchange

WORDS & PHRASES

Information desk

Currency Exchange

Exchange rate

Application for exchange

Local currency

Cash

Check

T/C(Traveler's Check)

Bill

Coin

Change

Cent

Nickel

Quarter

Half dollar

Bank teller

Single

BASIC EXPRESSIONS

- Is there a money exchange around here?
- Where can I change some money?
- What's the exchange rate for won?
- One dollar is equivalent to 1,100 won.
- Today's rate is about 1,050 won to the dollar.
- How much do you want to exchange?
- How would you like your money?
- How would you like it?
- I'd like all 20 dollars bills.

▲ 환전하기

CONVERSATIONS

Currency exchange: Dialogue ①

A : I'd like to cash this traveler's check.

B : Well, how would you like the money?

A : Two ten dollar bills, two fives*, four quarters, and make the remainder** singles***.

B : Would you sign here, please?

A : Yes. Here it is.

---

* two five dollar bills: 5달러짜리 2장

** remainer: 나머지

*** singles: single은 1달러. singles는 1달러짜리 여러개를 말한다.

Translation 우리말 해석을 보며 영어표현을 다시 연습한다.

A : 이 여행자 수표를 현금으로 바꾸고 싶습니다.

B : 얼마짜리 돈으로 바꾸어 드릴까요?

A : 10달러 지폐 두장, 5달러짜리 두 장, 25센트 동전 네 개, 그리고 나머지는 1달러짜리로 주십시오.

B : 여기에 서명해 주십시오.

A : 네. 여기 있습니다.

Currency exchange: Dialogue ②

A : Can I exchange Korean money for U.S. dollars?

B : Yes. How much would you like to exchange?

A : What's the exchange rate of won to the dollar?

B : As of today, 1,200 won per dollar.

A : Could I have change* for a twenty dollar bill?

B : Sure. How would you like the change?

* 여기서 change는 '바꾸다'라는 뜻이 아니라 '잔돈'의 의미로 쓰여 항상 단수로 쓰인다.

Translation

우리말 해석을 보며 영어표현을 다시 연습한다.

A : 한국 돈을 달러로 바꿀 수 있을까요?

B : 네. 얼마나 바꾸시겠습니까?

A : 달러에 대한 원화의 환율이 어떻게 됩니까?

B : 오늘 현재 1달러당 1,200원입니다.

A : 20달러 지폐를 잔돈으로 바꾸어 주실 수 있습니까?

B : 물론입니다. 얼마짜리로 바꾸어 드릴까요?

Currency exchange: Dialogue ③

A : Excuse me, where can I change some money?

B : Currency Exchange? Go to the second floor and turn right. There are three money exchanges.

A : Thanks a lot.

A : I'd like to change some Korean money into dollars.

C : Sure. How much would you like to change?

A : 1.5 million won, please.

Translation

우리말 해석을 보며 영어표현을 다시 연습한다.

A : 죄송하지만 어디서 환전할 수 있나요?

B : 환전소요? 이층에 가시면 왼쪽에 있는데요. 환전소가 3개 있습니다.

A : 감사합니다.

A : 한국 돈을 달러로 바꿔 주세요.

C : 네, 얼마를 바꿔드릴까요?

A : 150만원이요.

▲ 해바라기는 행운과 부의 상징~^^

FURTHER EXPRESSIONS

1. Can you tell me today's exchange rate?

2. It's 1,050 Won to one US Dollar.

3. Money exchange at the airport stays open 24 hours.

4. How much would you like to exchange, ma'am?

5. We provide exchange service for the seven notified foreign currencies.

6. Please fill out this form.

7. Please sign here.

8. Check the amount, please.

9. Please keep the receipt,

10. Where can I cash checks?

11. You can cash checks at the bank counter on the second floor.

TASK

❶ 인터넷에서 주요 국가별 원화 대비 환율을 알아보자.

❷ 가까운 은행에 가서 환전에 관한 정보를 알아보자.

Memo

Travel by Air Tips

Finding discount plane tickets and cheap tours is only the first step to traveling abroad. Once you arrive at your destination, what things would you expect to do when passing through immigration and customs in a foreign country?

▲ Nowadays, global travel is commonplace for pleasure or business; however, be sure to check with your airline about items that you shouldn't carry in your luggage. Otherwise, you might have to give them up.

▲ New Zealand 휴양지 Wanaka 의 촉촉한 거리 풍경.

Part 2

Staying at A Hotel

Unit 6

Ground Transportation

WORDS & PHRASES

Driver's license

Traffic regulation

Against the law

Fare

Take the subway

Rush hour

Quite a distance

Transfer

Conductor

Heavy traffic

Take me to 31st street.

Take me to 7th avenue.

Coach

Prohibited

Put in

Slot

Push through

Turnstile

Get off

BASIC EXPRESSIONS

- What is the bus fare?
- It's my first time to take the subway.
- Smoking in the coaches is prohibited.
- Which is the quickest way to get to Lake Park?
- You'd better take the subway.
- Put the ticket in the slot and push through the turnstile
- You've come too far.
- It's quite a distance from here.
- Please take me to the International airport.
- Can I get off at the subway station?
- Do not get off until the bus has stopped.
- You must get off at the next stop and transfer.
- May I have a transfer?

CONVERSATIONS

Dialogue ①

A : Excuse me, I'd like some information* about transportation.

B : Okay.

A : How do I get to downtown Atlanta?

B : You can take any one of these: taxi, airport bus, shuttle bus or limousine.

A : What is the best way to go?

B : I'd take the shuttle bus.

---

* Information은 항상 단수형태로 쓰인다. 정보는 '수'가 아니라 '양'으로 측정하기 때문이다.
  ex) A book ↔ Some books
  A piece of information ↔ some information

Translation 우리말 해석을 보며 영어표현을 다시 연습한다.

A : 실례지만, 교통편을 좀 물어 보고 싶은데요.

B : 네, 그러세요.

A : 애틀란타 시내까지 가려면 어떻게 가면 됩니까?

B : 택시, 공항버스, 셔틀버스, 리무진 중에서 탈 수 있습니다.

A : 어느 것을 타고 가면 가장 좋을까요?

B : 저 같으면 셔틀 버스를 타겠습니다.

Dialogue ❷

A : Can I get a city map here?

B : No. This is the airport information desk.

You can get* one at the tourist information desk.

A : How much does it cost to go downtown by taxi?

B : More than 40 dollars.

A : Will it be hard to get a hotel room without a reservation?

B : I don't think so. As it's not high season, it will be easy to get one** at this time of year.***

---

* get은 '얻다' (obtain)의 뜻.

** a hotel room

*** at this time of year: 연 중 이맘 때

Translation 우리말 해석을 보며 영어표현을 다시 연습한다.

A : 시내 지도를 얻을 수 있을까요?

B : 여기는 공항 안내소라서 지도가 없습니다.
관광 안내소에 가시면 얻을 수 있습니다.

A : 택시로 시내까지 가려면 요금이 얼마나 나옵니까?

B : 40달러 이상 나옵니다.

A : 예약이 없으면 호텔 방을 구하기가 어려울까요?

B : 제 생각엔 그렇지 않습니다. 지금 비수기라서 연 중 이 맘 때면 방 구하기가 쉬울 겁니다.

Dialogue ❸

A : Will this bus take me to Georgia Tech*?

B : Yes, but what part of Georgia Tech do you wish to go to?

A : I want to go to the International Language Institute.

B : OK, get on** now.

A : Thanks. How many more stops do I have to go?

B : Just 3 stops from here. I'll let you know when you get*** there.

---

* 미국 Georgia 주 Atlanta 도심(downtown)에 위치한 유명한 공과대학 Georgia Institute of Technology. 줄여서 Georgia Tech이라 부른다. Campus가 넓어 trolley 라고 부르는 노란 버스가 학교 안에서 운행되고 있다.

** get on 은 버스에 올라 타다, Taxi 같은 경우는 get in, hop in 등을 쓴다. 차에서 '내리다'는 모두 get off.

*** 여기서 'get'은 도착하다 (arrive)의 뜻.

Translation

우리말 해석을 보며 영어표현을 다시 연습한다.

A : 이 버스 조지아텍 가나요?

B : 네, 조지아텍 어디 가시나요?

A : 국제어학원에 가려고 합니다.

B : 네, 타세요.

A : 감사합니다. 몇 정거장 가야 하나요?

B : 여기서 세 정거장 이예요. 도착하면 알려드릴께요.

FURTHER EXPRESSIONS

1. May I see your driver's license?

2. What's the matter, officer?

3. You can't make a U-turn here.

4. You broke a traffic regulation.

5. It's against the law.

6. Watch the signs carefully and don't do it again.

7. I see, officer.

8. How much is the fare, driver?

9. That'll be $4.50.

10. Here's a 20$ bill.

11. Don't you have anything smaller?

12. We have to wait for the light to turn green.

TASK

❶ 한국을 비롯한 세계의 5개국을 자유로이 선택하여 전철, 버스, 택시 등의 대중교통의 요금을 Internet에서 찾아 영어로 정리하고 발표해보자.

❷ 자동차 운전석이 우리와 다른 쪽에 있는 나라들은 어느나라인지 조사해 보자.

❸ 또한 1번에서 조사한 5개 각 나라의 자동차 연료인 Gasoline(Oil) 가격은 어떻게 차이가 나는지 살펴보자.

Memo

Unit 7

Hotel Reservations

WORDS & PHRASES

Reserve

Book

Make a room reservation

Accommodation

Reservation desk

Put up

Available, Availability

Single room, double room

Twin room, Suite room.

Rate, Charge

Initial

Spell

Travel agency

Confirm

Vacancy

Moderate

Recommend

Hold

BASIC EXPRESSIONS

- Could you reserve a hotel room for me?
- I'd like to make a room reservation.
- I'd like to get a hotel room.
- Can I put up at your hotel?
- Is there a room available?
- Do you have any rooms available?
- What kind (type) of room would you like?
- What accommodation do you require?
- I'd like to book a single room.
- How long are you going to stay?
- What is the rate? How much do you charge?
- It's 85 dollars per night.
- Aren't there any rooms available on the first floor?
- How do you spell your name?
- What time would you like to check in?
- Hold the room for me, please.

CONVERSATIONS

Dialogue ①

A : Hilton Hotel. What can I do for you*?

B : Yes. I'd like to make a reservation for tonight. Is there a single room available**?

A : Yes, we have vacancies***. What time would you like to check in?

B : I should be there in three hours. How much do you charge****?

A : A single room with a bath is 70 dollars a night.

B : Okay. I'll take it. Please hold the room for me.

---

* May I help you?, How may I help you? 와 같은 뜻.
** available: 예약 가능한, 할 수 있는.
*** vacancies: 비어있는 방들 (vacant rooms)
**** charge: 금액을 청구하다, 부과하다.

Translation

우리말 해석을 보며 영어표현을 다시 연습한다.

A : 힐튼 호텔입니다. 무얼 도와 드릴까요?

B : 네. 오늘 밤에 묵을 방을 예약하고 싶은데요. 사용가능한 싱글 룸 있습니까?

A : 네, 빈 방이 있습니다. 몇 시에 투숙하시겠습니까?

B : 세 시간 후에 도착하게 될 겁니다. 숙박료는 얼마나 되나요?

A : 욕실이 달린 1인용 방은 하룻밤에 70달러입니다.

B : 좋습니다. 투숙하겠어요. 그 방을 내 앞으로 예약해 주세요.

▲ Hilton Hotel

Dialogue ②

A : I'd like to reserve a room for a couple of weeks starting tonight.

B : What type of room would you like, sir?

A : I'd like a suite room*.

B : What time would you like to check in?

A : I'll be there in 50 minutes. I've just arrived at the airport from Korea.

▲ Suite room

* suite: 침실, 욕실에 이어 응접실이 달린 한벌의 방. 음악에서는 모음곡(조곡)의 뜻

Translation 우리말 해석을 보며 영어표현을 다시 연습한다.

A : 오늘 밤부터 한 이주일 동안 머물 방을 하나 예약하고 싶습니다.

B : 어떤 방을 원하십니까?

A : 스위트 룸이요.

B : 몇 시에 투숙하시겠습니까?

A : 50분 후에 가겠습니다. 한국에서 이곳 공항에 지금 막 도착했습니다.

FURTHER EXPRESSIONS

1. Can I book a twin room for tonight?

2. I'm afraid we're completely booked up.

3. Can I reserve a hotel room from here?

4. What kind of hotel do you have in mind, ma'am?

5. I'd like a moderately priced one. You know, what they call 'an economy hotel.'

6. What price range do you have in mind?

7. I want to stay under 100 dollars per night.

8. I'll check on it for you.

9. I've arrived here without a hotel reservation.

10. Could you recommend a good place to stay downtown?

11. Will it be possible to get a hotel room in town?

12. There should be plenty of vacancies at this time.

TASK

❶ Internet에서 유명 호텔을 검색하여 방가격(room rate)과 부대시설 (facilities)을 알아보자.

❷ 호텔과 비행기 등을 미리 예약 해서 할인하여 살 수 있는 판매를 영어로 무엇이라고 하는가?

Memo

Unit 8

Checking-in / Checking-out

Words & Phrases

Check–in

Check–out

Have a reservation

Vacancies

Fully booked

Available

Recommend

Stationery

Brochures

Room charge

Payment

Double–check

Receipt

Change

BASIC EXPRESSIONS

- I'd like to check in.
- I have a reservation.
- Let me check if we have any vacancies.
- Sorry we're fully booked.
- You have to find another hotel.
- We don't have any rooms available.
- I'll get you a room reservation at another hotel.
- How long are you planning to stay?
- Let me guide you to your room. This way, please.
- After you, please.
- Is this your first visit to our hotel?
- Thank for choosing our hotel and staying with us.
- One of my friends recommended this to me.
- This is your room, 2332. Your room has a very nice view of the beach.
- The stationery and hotel brochures are here.
- Please wear this gas mask in case of fire.
- You pull this to operate the bathroom showers.
- Please ask our room maid for laundry to go out for dry cleaning.

- I hope you'll enjoy your stay here.
- Please return your room key here when you check-out.
- If you check-out after 12:30 pm an overcharge will be added to your bill.
- You can only use this meal coupon in the designated restaurant.
- Did you pay for your room charge at your travel agency?

▲ 파리의 몽마르트 언덕

CONVERSATIONS

Checking-in: Dialogue ❶

A : Hello, Hilton Hotel. May I help you?

B : Yes. I'd like to check in. I have a reservation at your hotel tonight. My name is Ms. Kim.

A : Just a moment. I'll check. Your reservation is for a single room for 3 nights starting today.

B : That's right.

A : Could you fill out this registration card*, Ma'am?

B : Sure, here you are.

A : Here's your room key. Your room is 1503.
Our bell man will carry your baggage.**

B : Thank you.

A : My pleasure.

---

* 숙박 등록카드에 기입(fill out 또는 fill in) 해주시겠습니까?

** baggage는 항상 단수형. luggage도 같은 뜻으로 항상 단수.

Translation 우리말 해석을 보며 영어표현을 다시 연습한다.

A : 힐튼 호텔입니다. 무엇을 도와 드릴까요?

B : 네. 이 호텔에 투숙하려고 합니다. 오늘 밤으로 예약했고 이름은 Ms. Kim 입니다.

A : 잠깐 만요. 확인해 보겠습니다. 오늘부터 3일간 싱글 룸으로 예약되어 있으십니다.

B : 맞습니다.

A : 숙박등록 신청서 작성 해주시기 바랍니다.

B : 네, 여기 있습니다.

A : 방 열쇠입니다. 1503호실입니다. 사환이 짐을 들어다 드릴 겁니다.

B : 감사합니다.

A : 천만에요.

Checking-in: Dialogue ❷

A : I'm going to be arriving there late for check–in. Will you hold my reservation, please?

B : Okay. We'll hold it.

A : My plane was delayed, so I'm running late. Please hold my reservation.

B : How late will you be?

A : If I'm going to be later than eight o'clock, I'll call again.

B : Okay, I hope there's no more delay than that.

Translation 우리말 해석을 보며 영어표현을 다시 연습한다.

A : 늦게 투숙하러 가게 될 것 같은데 예약을 그대로 유지시켜 주시겠습니까?

B : 네. 그러겠습니다.

A : 비행기가 연착해서 늦어지겠습니다. 예약을 그대로 유지해 주시기 바랍니다.

B : 얼마나 늦어질 것 같습니까?

A : 8시보다 더 늦어질 것 같으면 다시 전화하겠습니다

B : 알겠습니다. 더 늦지 않으시기를 바랍니다.

Checking-out: Dialogue ①

A : I'd like to check out now. Here's my room key.

B : Thanks. How would you like to make your payment, sir?
In cash or with credit card?

A : By credit card. Here's my Master card.

B : Thanks. The total comes to 270 dollars. Sign here, please.

A : Okay, here it is.

B : Thank you. Hope you enjoyed your stay with us.

Translation 우리말 해석을 보며 영어표현을 다시 연습한다.

A : 퇴실하려 합니다. 방 열쇠 여기 있습니다.

B : 감사. 어떻게 지불하실 건가요? 현금, 신용카드?

A : 신용카드로 할께요. 비자 카드 여기 있습니다.

B : 감사합니다. 총 270불입니다. 서명해 주세요.

A :네. 여기 있습니다.

B : 감사합니다. 저희 호텔에서 즐겁게 지내셨기를 바랍니다.

Checking-out: Dialogue ❷

A : Are you checking out now?

B : Yes, room 423. How much would that be?

A : It comes to 320 dollars. How would you like to pay?

B : Cash, please.

A : Here's your receipt and change. Let me find an envelope for you.

B : Thanks. I really enjoyed staying here. Bye.

Translation 우리말 해석을 보며 영어표현을 다시 연습한다.

A : 퇴실하시겠습니까?

B : 네. 423호요. 얼마 나왔나요?

A : 320불입니다. 어떻게 계산하시겠어요?

B : 현금이요.

A : 영수증과 잔돈입니다. 봉투에 넣어드리겠습니다.

B : 감사합니다. 여기서 지내는 동안 즐거웠습니다. 안녕히~

FURTHER EXPRESSIONS

1. Welcome to our hotel. Let me guide you to the front desk. This way, please.
2. I'm afraid we don't have any rooms available tonight.
3. We have a special check-in desk for suite room guests for your convenience.
4. Thank you for visiting our hotel. I'm sure you will be satisfied with our hotel.
5. Please check your baggage.
6. Are you checking out?
7. Have you taken anything from the refrigerator?
8. Are you using the safety deposit box?
9. Today's exchange rate is 1050 won per US dollar.
10. You have exceeded your check-out time by 2 hours. Therefore, you have to pay an extra charge of 20 %.
11. Do you have another card?
12. This card is invalid.

13. Your card has exceeded its monthly amount limit.

14. You have made partial payment before.

15. Please double check this.

16. Your phone bill will be automatically added to your bill.

17. Would you endorse this check, please?

18. I'll deduct the miscalculated amount from your statement.

19. Hope you'll enjoy your trip, ma'am. Thank you and goodbye!

▲ 한가로운 뉴질랜드 휴양지 Wanaka의 예쁜 크림색 집.

TASK

❶ 호텔에 투숙할 때 확인해야 할 사항은 무엇인가?

❷ 호텔에서 퇴실할 때 확인하고 준비해야 할 사항은 무엇인가?

❸ 호텔 에는 어떠한 부대시설들이 기본적이고 필수적인지 임의로 7개의 호텔을 골라 살펴보자.

Memo

Unit 9

House Keeping / At the Restaurant

Words & Phrases

Housekeeping service

Room Service

Send someone up

Maid

Laundry

Have the letter mailed

Pull the shade (blind, shield) up (down)

Damp season, Moldy

Sewer (Drainage) clogged

Washed off

Inside out

Sewed up

These need dry-cleaning.

Have shirt mended

Have button fixed

Extra bath towel

Restaurant

Make an order

Take an order

Have it changed

Sauce, Dressing

Reception

Make a reservation for two

Book a table for three

Menu

Appetizer

Main dish

Dessert

Another helping

Extra portion

Overdone, Undercooked

Recommend

Suggestion

Keep the change

BASIC EXPRESSIONS

Housekeeping

- Send a maid to my room, please.
- I'd like my room cleaned.
- My room number is 332.
- Where can I get it back?
- If rushed, there is an extra charge.
- I want an extra bath gown, towel, and pillow.
- I'll have it sent up to your room right away.
- My room is just in a mess.
- Repair, alteration, etc. wanted
- Do you want this washing to go out?
- Quick service, regular service
- Please sign the laundry slip.
- Things are moldy in the damp area.
- Sewer is clogged.
- Water is running.

Restaurant

- I'd like to make a reservation for three.
- I want to reserve a table for two.
- I'd like to book a table for three.
- Your table for three is prepared now.
- What would you like to order?
- Are you ready to order?
- I'd like to take your order.
- May I take your order?
- We served breakfast at 7:30 to 9AM.
- What would you like (to have) for breakfast?
- What would you recommend for us?
- What's good on the menu this morning?
- What is your special today?
- I'd like to have breakfast in my room.
- What time do you want breakfast served?
- I'd like to order roast beef,
- Would you care for a cocktail?

Conversations

Housekeeping: Dialogue ①

A : Housekeeping, may I help you?

B : Please send a maid* to my room.

A : What is your room number?

B : It's 432. I'd like the room cleaned** up.

A : Yes, sir. The maid will be there in no time.
Is there anything else?

B : I have some shirts to be washed.***
If I send out laundry today, when can I get them back?

A : Usually, you can get them the next day.
Are you in a hurry?

B : Yes, I am.

---

* room maid: 호텔 객실 청소직원.

** 방이 치워지는 것이니 수동의 의미로 과거분사 (past participle) 형태인 'cleaned'를 사용한다.

*** 세탁이 되어진다는 의미로 역시 p.p형태 'washed'가 쓰임.

Translation 우리말 해석을 보며 영어표현을 다시 연습한다.

A : 객실 관리입니다. 무얼 도와드릴까요?

B : 객실 청소 하시는 분 보내주세요.

A : 몇 호실 이신가요?

B : 432 호입니다. 방 청소 해주세요.

A : 알겠습니다. 곧 청소하시는 분이 가실 겁니다.
다른 건 없으신지요?

B : 세탁해야 할 셔츠가 몇 벌 있습니다.
오늘 세탁 맡기면, 언제 찾을 수 있나요?

A : 보통 다음날 찾을 수 있습니다.
급하신 건가요?

B : 네, 그렇습니다.

Housekeeping: Dialogue ❷

A : Housekeeping, Can I help you?

B : Yes, please. This is Ms. Kim in room 505.

The toilet is overflowing* now.

A : I'm terribly sorry about that. We'll send a plumber** right up there to fix it.

B : And the television isn't working, either.

A : I'm very sorry for the inconvenience***.

I'll call maintenance**** immediately and have it fixed for you.

---

* overflow: 흘러 넘치다.

** plumber: 배관공

*** inconvenience: 불편함

**** maintenance: 관리, 보수부서

Translation 우리말 해석을 보며 영어표현을 다시 연습한다.

A : 객실 관리입니다. 무얼 도와드릴까요?

B : 505 호실의 미즈 김인데요. 변기 물이 넘치고 있어요.

A : 정말 죄송합니다. 배관공을 바로 올려 보내서 고치도록 하겠습니다.

B : 텔레비전도 작동이 안됩니다.

A : 불편을 끼쳐드려 정말 죄송합니다. 즉시 관리부서에 전화해서 고치도록 하겠습니다.

Restaurant: Dialogue ①

A : Do you have a table for three?

B : Yes, we do. Come this way, please.

A : Thanks. The table by the window looks very good.

B : Indeed, sir! Are you ready to order now?

A : Yes, what would you recommend?

B : Sirloin* steak is today's special.

A : OK, then we'll have three sirloin steaks.

* Sirloin: 등심, 부드러운 안심은 tenderloin.

Translation

우리말 해석을 보며 영어표현을 다시 연습한다.

A : 3인용 테이블 자리 있나요?

B : 네. 있습니다. 이리로 오시지요.

A : 감사합니다. 창가 옆 테이블이 아주 좋네요.

B : 정말 그렇습니다. 선생님. 주문하시겠습니까?

A : 네, 뭘 추천하시나요?

B : 등심 스테이크가 오늘의 특별요리 입니다.

A : 알겠습니다. 그럼 등심 스테이크로 3인분 주세요.

Restaurant: Dialogue ②

A : How would you like your steak?

B : 2 medium, and 1 well-done, please.

A : Would you like to order dessert?

B : Yes, What do you have for dessert?

A : We have waffle with cream and chocolate, and fresh fruits.

B : I'll have fresh fruits.

Translation 우리말 해석을 보며 영어표현을 다시 연습한다.

A : 스테이크를 어떻게 해 드릴까요?

B : 둘은 중간, 하나는 잘 익혀서 주세요.

A : 후식 주문 하시겠습니까?

B : 네. 후식에는 뭐가 있나요?

A : 크림과 초코렛 곁들인 와플, 그리고 신선한 과일입니다.

B : 신선한 과일로 먹을께요.

FURTHER EXPRESSIONS

1. I'd like something not so heavy.

2. How about spaghetti for lunch?

3. Is it delicious?

4. What kind of sauce do you like?

5. Cream cheese sauce, please.

6. Would you like some salad?

7. What kind of dressing do you have?

8. Thousand Island, French and Italian dressing.

9. Do you have a reservation, sir?

10. Is there a table available for three people?

11. I'm sorry, we have no tables available at this moment.

12. I don't mind waiting.

13. Did you enjoy your meal?

14. The vegetable soup was delicious.

15. May I have the bill?

16. 10% service charge and 10% value added tax (VAT) are included on your bill.

17. Do you take credit cards?

18. Of course, we do.

19. Here's my card.

20. Thank you very much. Sign here, please.

◀ Pumpkin soup and bread for breakfast

▲ A cup of long black coffee, a pot of tea, and delicious scones with fresh berry jam & cheese at the Cafe, Sweethearts in CHCH, NZ.

TASK

❶ 가장 좋아하는 음식(your favorite food) 을 선택해서 영어로 recipe를 만들어 발표해 보자.

❷ Fast food 점이나 Coffee shop에 가서 영어로 주문해 보자.

❸ Internet에서 간단한 soup recipe를 검색하여 만들어 보고 그 과정을 영어로 써 보자.

Memo

Unit 10

Shopping

WORDS & PHRASES

Souvenir

Owe

Cash

Charge

Accept credit cards

Traveler's check

Change, Short–changed

Expensive

Overcharge

Come down

Cheap

Lowest price

Reasonable

Within one's budget

Receipt

Refund

ID (Identification Card)

BASIC EXPRESSIONS

- I'd like to buy some souvenirs.
- I'm looking for something as a souvenir.
- How much do I owe you?
- How much does it cost?
- What is the price of it?
- It is 35 dollars.
- That will be 25 dollars.
- Do you take credit cards?
- We take major credit cards.
- How about traveler's checks?
- Could you show me your I.D., ma'am?
- May I see your passport, sir?
- That's too expensive.
- Could you show me a cheaper one?
- It's the lowest price we can offer.
- It's reasonable.
- You're overcharging me.
- Can you come down a little?

Conversations

Dialogue 1

A : I'm looking for something as a souvenir.

How much is this*?

B : One hundred and ten dollars, ma'am..

A : That's too expensive.

I think you are overcharging** me.

B : No, ma'am. That's the lowest price I can offer you.

A : Can you come down*** a little?

I have to stay within my budget****.

B : Okay, I'll give you a 3 percent discount.

---

* what's the price of this?, How much do I owe you? 와 같은 뜻.
** overcharge: 지나치게 값을 부르다. 바가지 씌우다.
*** come down: 값을 내리다. 깍아 주다.
**** within one's budget: 예산 범위 내에서

Translation 우리말 해석을 보며 영어표현을 다시 연습한다.

A : 기념품이 될 만한 것을 찾고 있습니다. 이거 얼마죠?

B : 110달러입니다.

A : 너무 비쌉니다. 값을 너무 지나치게 부르시는군요.

B : 아닙니다. 최저 가격을 말씀드린 겁니다.

A : 조금 값을 내려 주시겠어요? 예산에 맞춰야 해서요.

B : 좋습니다. 3 퍼센트 깎아 드리죠.

▲ A souvenir from Arrowtown in NZ.

Dialogue ❷

A : How much do I owe you?

B : That'll be 30 dollars and 50 cents.

A : Do you accept credit cards?

B : Yes. We take all major credit cards.

A : How about traveler's checks?

B : Of course we accept them. But we need to see your I.D., ma'am.

▲ 기념품 (souvenir) 으로 좋은, 기모노 입은 화려한 일본의 전통 인형들. 다소 비싼 것이 흠이다.

Translation 우리말 해석을 보며 영어표현을 다시 연습한다.

A : 얼마입니까?

B : 30달러 50센트입니다.

A : 신용 카드도 받습니까?

B : 네. 주요 신용 카드를 다 받습니다.

A : 여행자 수표도 받습니까?

B : 물론 받습니다. 신분증명서를 보여 주셔야 합니다.

▲ Arrowtown, NZ의 가을축제에서 만난 세계적인 가구 디자이너의 꼬마 의자들~

Dialogue ③

A : Could you look at this receipt again, please?

B : Is there anything wrong, sir?

A : You gave me the wrong change.

B : I don't think I did.

A : I think there's a mistake with this bill.

B : Which part of the bill are you disagreeing with?

▲ 전화기, 자명종 시계 등 잡화를 파는 souvenir shop.

Translation 우리말 해석을 보며 영어표현을 다시 연습한다.

A : 이 영수증을 다시 한 번 봐 주시겠어요?

B : 뭐가 잘못된 것이 있습니까?

A : 거스름돈을 잘못 주신 것 같은데요.

B : 그럴 리가 없을 텐데요.

A : 이 계산서에 뭔가 실수가 있는 것 같은데요.

B : 어떤 점이 이상하십니까?

FURTHER EXPRESSIONS

1. What seems to be the problem?

2. It doesn't work* properly.

3. Let me check to see what is wrong with it.

4. Here's the receipt.

5. Here is your change.

6. Would you mind checking the bill again?

7. Is there anything wrong with the bill?

8. I think I was short-changed.**

9. I'd like a refund*** on this.

---

* work properly 는 제대로 작동하다. 여기서는 doesn't 가 있으니 작동이 제대로 되지 않다는 뜻.

** 거스름 돈을 덜 받다.

*** 환불

10. Please endorse this check.

11. Keep the receipt, please.

12. Could you give me a discount?

▲ 미국 영화배우 제임스 딘의 포스터가 있는 다양한 상품을 파는 NZ의 한 앤틱(antique) 상점.

▲ 이탈리아 베니스

TASK

❶ 해외여행 기념품으로 알맞은 상품과 가격에 대해 각 나라 별로 알아보고 토론해 보자.

❷ 합리적인 가격이란 무엇인가?

❸ 현명한 쇼핑습관은 어떤 것인지 토론해 보자.

Memo

Life is a song worth singing!

▲ Akaroa Harbour, NZ. Beautiful~

All's well that ends well!

저자약력

강 명 재

- 여주대 비즈니스영어과 교수

- 홍익대 박사 (응용언어학)
- 미국 위스콘신 주립대 (River-Falls) 석사 (영어교육)
- 상명여자 사범대학교 (영어교육과)

- 현) BBB 영어통역 봉사요원
- 전) Korea TESOL 회장
- 전) 상명대, 홍익대, 강남대 강사

English for TRAVELING Abroad

2011년 7월 20일 초판1쇄 발행
2014년 2월 10일 초판3쇄 발행

저 자 강 명 재
펴낸이 임 순 재
펴낸곳 **한올출판사**

등록 제11-403호
121-849
주 소 서울시 마포구 성산동 133-3 한올빌딩 3층
전 화 (02)376-4298(대표)
팩 스 (02)302-8073
홈페이지 www.hanol.co.kr
e-메 일 hanol@hanol.co.kr
정 가 15,000원

저자와의 협의하에 인지생략

▫ ISBN 978-89-94948-28-7